60 Gluten-Free
Easy Recipes

Katharine Jackson

Introduction

I want to thank you and congratulate you for purchasing the book, *"60 Gluten-Free Recipes"*.

This book contains 60 tasty gluten free recipes that you have to try today.

What do you think or imagine when you hear the word gluten-free? Most people think that now that they want to adopt a gluten free diet, they need to say "bye bye" to the pastries they love and other goodies that are made from wheat since as we know, wheat has gluten and it is a no-no when on a gluten-free diet. However, just because you cannot take wheat, rye, barley and other grain does not mean that you cannot have amazing and tasty meals.

You will be amazed that there are many substitutes you can use in place of the foods that may have gluten. Furthermore, you will not even notice such a huge difference in the foods. In any case, you will be eating healthy owing to the very many negative effects of the protein gluten.

60 Gluten-Free Easy Recipes

This book will open your eyes to all the amazing gluten-free recipes that you can enjoy. With the recipes in this book, you will not feel deprived because you cannot have your favorite cake. Actually, you would be able to bake your favorite cake the difference only being the substitute ingredients you will use. That aside, with the recipes in this book, I assure you that you will actually be excited to start trying out the recipes and in no time, you will discover that all your meals are gluten-free and they actually taste really good.

Thanks again for purchasing this book, I hope you enjoy it!

Table of Contents

Why Go Gluten-Free?

Unless you are not living in this world, chances are that you have heard about the word, "gluten". However, do you know what gluten is, where gluten is found, why the need to embrace a gluten-free diet and what are some gluten-free foods? Most people have these and many more questions but before we can know where you can find gluten, it is prudent that you first understand what gluten is. Gluten is simply a kind of protein that is found in wheat and other grains like barley, triticale and rye. It is the glue-like substance that holds food together. Haven't you noticed how a mixture of wheat flour and water is very sticky? This is the work of gluten.

Most people suffering from celiac disease, a condition where the lining of the small intestine is damaged as a result of a reaction from eating gluten do not have an option but not to eat anything that may have gluten. While we all agree that people suffering from celiac disease need to stay away from gluten, what if you do not suffer from celiac disease; how can you benefit from embracing a gluten free diet? Eating gluten is linked to several conditions like leaky gut, inflammation of the digestive tract as well as weight gain. Thus, you can benefit greatly from eating a gluten free diet. Below is a list of foods to avoid:

*Barley

*Rye

*Wheat products like durum flour, bulgur, faina, semolina, spelt and kamut

Other foods to avoid unless indicated 'gluten free' include breads, gravies, French fries, cakes and pies, cereals, candies, beer, self-basting poultry, seasoned snack foods, pastas and vegetables in sauces.

Let's look at some of the recipes you can try out.

Gluten Free Breakfast Recipes

1. Bacon and Egg Cups

Bacon and Egg Cups

Servings: 3

Ingredients

6 slices of bacon

6 eggs

1 ounce cheese (not compulsory)

Salt and pepper

Directions

Heat the oven up to 350 degrees F and using a cupcake pan, line the holes with a bacon slice while pressing the bacon on the edges of the hole. Crack and pour an egg into each hole then sprinkle with salt and pepper with cheese if you wish. Bake for 20 minutes at 350 degrees. The bacon and egg cups will pop out of the cupcake pan once done.

2. Gluten-Free Waffles

Gluten-Free Waffles

Servings: 5

Ingredients

½ cup of potato starch

1 cup of brown rice or rice flour

1 teaspoon table salt

¼ cup of oil

2 teaspoons of baking powder

2 eggs (optional)

¼ cup of tapioca flour

1 teaspoon sugar

1 ½ cups of milk (butter milk preferred)

Directions

Whisk all the above ingredients together then pour the mixture into a waffle iron in bunches. If too runny, add some rice flour or milk if it is too thick. If made without eggs then you will need to add a little more liquid to substitute them. Bake until the steaming stops.

3. Lemon Poppy Seed Muffins

Lemon Poppy Seed Muffins

Servings: 3

Ingredients

¼ cup of coconut flour

3 eggs

¼ cup of agave nectar

¼ teaspoon of lemon zest

¼ teaspoon of baking soda

¼ teaspoon of Celtic sea salt

¼ cup of grape seed

1 tablespoon of poppy seeds

1 tablespoon of lemon zest

Directions

Combine salt, coconut flour and baking soda in a medium bowl then mix agave, lemon zest, oil and eggs in a another bowl. Blend dry ingredients into the wet ones then fold in poppy seeds. Smoother 1 tablespoon batter into every greased mini muffin and bake for 8-10 minutes at 350 degrees F. Allow to cool and serve.

4. Spicy Tomato Baked Eggs

Spicy Tomato Baked Eggs

Servings: 2

Ingredients

1 tablespoon olive oil

1 red chili, finely chopped and deseeded

2 chopped red onions

1 sliced garlic clove

4 eggs

2 (400g) cans tomato cherries

Small size coriander with stalks and leaves separately chopped

1 teaspoon caster sugar

Directions

Heat olive oil in a frying pan. Soften the onions, chili, coriander stalks and garlic. Once soft, add in the sugar and tomatoes then bubble the mix for 8-10 minutes until thick. Make 4 dips in the sauce using the back side of a large spoon then crack in an egg into each. Place a lid on the pan and allow cooking over low-heat for about 6-8 minutes until the eggs are done to your desired liking. Scatter in the coriander leaves and serve with some crusty bread.

5. Veggie Breakfast Bakes

Veggie Breakfast Bakes

Servings: 4

Ingredients

4 large mushrooms

1 thinly sliced garlic clove

8 halved tomatoes

200g bag of spinach

4 eggs

2 teaspoons olive oil

Directions

Preheat the oven to 200/180°c. Place the tomatoes and mushrooms into four ovenproof dishes and then divide garlic between the dishes. Add the oil and seasoning sparingly then bake for 10 minutes.

In the meantime, place the spinach in a wide colander them add a liter of boiling water for wilting. Squeeze out any retained water then add the spinach to each of the four dishes. Making a little gap in between the vegetables, crack an egg into each dish and return back into the oven to cook for an extra 8-10 minutes or until the egg cooks to your desired liking.

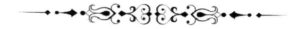

6. Orange Polentina

Orange Polentina

Servings: 3

Ingredients

1 medium size orange

1 ½ cups 2% low-fat milk

2 cups of clean water

¼ cup of Italian cream cheese

¾ cup of instant polenta or fine corn meal

¼ cup low-fat Greek yoghurt

¼ teaspoon salt

4 tablespoons honey

1 teaspoon fresh tarragon, finely chopped (if desired)

Directions

Zest the orange to derive 1 ½ teaspoons of zest then set aside. Using a sharp knife, remove the rest of the peel and the white pith. Cut the segments from the adjoining membranes and set aside for garnish. Mix water, salt and milk in a wide, heavy saucepan and boil. Sparingly add in the polenta and continue boiling. Set the heat to medium-low to maintain even bubbling and whisk until the polentina thickens, probably 1-5 minutes. Remove from heat, cover with a lid and allow cooling for 5 minutes.

In the meantime, mix yoghurt, mascarpone, a tablespoon of honey and ½ teaspoon of orange zest in a small size bowl. Add in the remaining, 3 tablespoons and 1 teaspoon of zest into the polentina. Divide between four bowls and top with a dollop of the cream cheese. Garnish with the orange pieces and sprinkle with tarragon. Serve immediately.

7. Banana Walnut Muffins

Banana Walnut Muffins

Servings: 2

Ingredients

3 eggs

¼ cup of coconut oil

¼ teaspoon Celtic salt

½ cup walnuts (toasted and chopped)

¼ cup coconut flour

3 pitted dates

2 bananas (medium)

½ teaspoon baking soda

10 drops of stevia

Directions

Place eggs, bananas, dates, stevia and oil in a blender and blend on medium speed until mixed then add coconut flour, baking soda and blend until smooth. Fold in walnuts, then scoop about ¼ cup batter into a muffin pan that's lined. Place in the oven and bake at 350 degrees F for about 20-25 minutes. Allow to cool and serve immediately.

8. Pumpkin Spice Muffins

Pumpkin Spice Muffins

Servings: 2

Ingredients

3 large eggs

½ teaspoon baking soda

1/8 teaspoon Celtic salt

1/8 teaspoon vanilla stevia

¼ cup of coconut flour

1 tablespoon ground ginger

1 tablespoon ground cinnamon

2 tablespoons palm shortening

½ cup of honey

½ cup of freshly roasted pumpkin (not canned)

Directions

Pulse together coconut flour, baking soda, salt, cinnamon and ginger in a food processor. Beat in the eggs, pumpkin, honey, stevia and shortening. Transfer this to a paper-lined muffin tin and bake for 25 minutes at 350 degrees F after which it is ready for serving.

Gluten Free Lunch Recipes

9. Rice noodles with sundried tomatoes, Parmesan & Basil

Rice noodles with sundried tomatoes, Parmesan & Basil

Servings: 4

Ingredients

25g shaved and grated parmesan cheese

85g sundried tomatoes

250g medium rice noodles

2 tablespoons dried tomato oil

Generous handful of basil leaves, torn

Directions

Prepare the packed noodles according to instructions and then drain them. Heat oil, add garlic and tomatoes and fry for about 2 minutes. Toss the noodles and a generous amount of basil and cheese into the pan, season then sprinkle remaining cheese and basil over the noodles. Serve while hot.

10. Vietnamese Rice-Noodle Salad

Vietnamese Rice-Noodle Salad

Servings: 44

Ingredients

5 cloves of garlic

½ jalapeno pepper, minced and seeded

1 cup chopped cilantro, loosely packed

3 tablespoons white sugar

3 tablespoons vegetarian fish sauce

2 julienned carrots

¼ cup chopped, fresh mint

¼ cup of unsalted peanuts

4 sprigs, fresh mint

¼ cup fresh lime juice

1 (12-ounce) package rice noodles

1 cucumber, cut into two and chopped

4 leaves of napa cabbage

Directions

Mince the cilantro with garlic and hot pepper and place the mix in a bowl. Add in the fish sauce, limejuice, salt and sugar and stir well then allow sauce to stand for 5 minutes. Boil salted water then add in the rice noodles, boil for 2 minutes then drain well. Rinse the noodles with some cold water to cool then allow them to drain again. Combine the sauce, cucumber, mint, carrots and napa cabbage in a wide serving bowl. Toss evenly and serve salad garnished with mint sprig and peanuts.

11. Corn-Tortilla Crusted Chicken Tenders

Corn-Tortilla Crusted Chicken Tenders

Servings: 4

Ingredients

12 chicken tenders (total of around 1 ½ pounds)

10 roughly torn corn tortillas

1 cup buttermilk

¼ cup coconut flour

Salt and pepper to taste

3 tablespoon honey

2 cups vegetable oil

3 tablespoons grainy mustard

Directions

Put tortillas in a food processor and blend until mixture looks like coarse meal, then season with pepper and salt then transfer to a medium-size bowl. Put the flour on a large plate and buttermilk in a shallow dish. Immerse chicken in flour allowing the excess to drip off then coat in buttermilk allowing excess to drip off then press in tortilla crumbs. Transfer to a baking sheet or large platter. Heat oil over medium heat in a large non-stick skillet and cook chicken thoroughly for about 12 minutes, flipping once until done and crust is golden. Transfer to wire rack or paper towels then set it over a rimmed baking sheet to drain any fluids. Combine honey and mustard in a small bowl and stir together until fully combined. Serve the chicken tenders with dip if desired.

12. Gluten–free Macaroni and Cheese

Gluten–free Macaroni and Cheese

Servings: 4

Ingredients

1 teaspoon Dijon mustard

2 tablespoons potato starch (gluten free)

3 tablespoons unsalted butter + more for dish

1 ounce (¼ cup) grated parmesan cheese

¾ gluten free penne, pounded, cooked, drained

¾ pound (3 cups) shredded cheddar

2 cups warmed, whole milk

½ cup slightly crushed crisp puffed rice cereal (gluten-free)

2 tablespoons potato starch

1 small, diced yellow onion

Coarse Salt and ground pepper

Directions

Preheat oven up to 350 degrees F then butter 2-quart baking dish or 8 oz ramekins then microwave 1 tablespoon butter until melted then toss with parmesan and cereal. In a medium-size saucepan over medium heat, melt 2 tablespoons butter, add onion and cook for about 4 minutes until softened. Sprinkle with potato starch and cook for a minute. Slowly stir in milk, stirring time to time until thickened for about 3 minutes. Remove from heat and stir in mustard and cheddar until smooth then season with pepper and salt. Add pasta and stir to coat then transfer to the baking dish or ramekins and sprinkle with the cereal mixture. Bake until the sauce is bubbling and topping turns golden, about 15-20 minutes.

13. Goat Cheese & Watercress Quiche

Goat Cheese & Watercress Quiche

Serves: 4

Ingredients

For pastry

100g butter

255g almond flour (or any gluten free flour like coconut flour, rice flour etc) plus 2 tablespoons for rolling

2 large size eggs (beaten)

For filling

150ml milk

150ml rindless goat's cheese (log soft, in rough chunks)

1 tablespoon oil

1 finely chopped, medium onion

100g roughly chopped watercress

2 large eggs

Freshly grated nutmeg (optional)

Directions

Pour the flour and a dash of salt in a large bowl then rub in butter until the mixture resembles breadcrumbs before stirring in 1-2 tablespoons water and one egg to form tender dough. Knead evenly then wrap and chill for about 30 minutes or more. Preheat oven to 200°C/ 180°F, knead pastry again and roll it out to border a 20cm flat pan (loose bottomed). Patch holes with remaining pastry brushing the sides and base with the second egg.

For the filling: Fry the onion in oil until soft then add watercress and cook until wilted. Add in the milk, beat in the eggs and stir in the goat's cheese and watercress combination. Season if desired, add a pinch of nutmeg, then place the flat pan on a baking sheet to bake for 5 minutes. Add the filling then bake for 15 more minutes. Reduce heat to 180°C and cook for about 25-30 minutes or till lightly set.

14. Parmesan Spinach Cakes

Parmesan Spinach Cakes

Servings: 4

Ingredients

½ cup low-fat cottage cheese or part-skim ricotta cheese

½ cup Parmesan cheese, finely shredded plus more to garnish

12 ounces fresh spinach

2 large beaten eggs

¼ teaspoon salt

¼ teaspoon pepper, freshly ground

1 minced, clove garlic

Directions

Preheat oven up to 400°F. Blend spinach in a food processor in 3 batches until finely chopped. Transfer to a medium size bowl, add Parmesan, eggs, ricotta, garlic, pepper and salt then stir to combine. Coat 8 muffin cups with cooking spray and divide the spinach into the 8 cups. Place the spinach cakes in the preheated oven and bake until set, about 20 minutes. Allow to cool for five minutes then loosen the edges with a knife and transfer onto a large plate or cutting board. Serve warm with shredded parmesan, if desired.

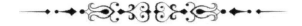

15. Lentil and Sweet-Potato Stew

Lentil and Sweet-Potato Stew

Servings: 6

Ingredients

2 tablespoons canola oil

1 bay leaf

2 peeled and chopped medium carrots

1 minced garlic clove.

1 medium, chopped onion (about 1 cup)

2 chopped medium, celery ribs

2 cups brown lentils (picked over, rinsed and dried)

2 medium size (1 pound) sweet potatoes peeled and sliced into ½ inch pieces.

½ cup fresh cilantro leaves, chopped

1 (14 ½ oz) can of diced tomatoes in juice

9 ounce (1 package) frozen cut green beans

Black pepper and coarse salt

1 ½ teaspoons curry powder

Low-fat yoghurt (plain), to serve

Directions

Heat oil in a large saucepan over medium-high heat. Add onions, celery, carrots and bay leaf then cook stirring for 5-7 minutes until the vegetables have softened. Add in garlic and curry powder and then cook for a minute or more until fragrant. Add in lentils and 7 cups of water then bring to a boil, reduce heat to simmer, cover to cook for 10 minutes. Add potatoes and continue cooking while covered until lentils and potatoes are just soft, about 15 minutes. Pour in tomatoes with juice and green beans and cook for 2-4 minutes until warmed through. Remove bay leaf and add the cilantro while seasoning with salt and pepper. Serve with yoghurt if desired.

16. Macaroni and Cheese 2

Macaroni and Cheese 2

Servings: 4-6

Ingredients

Salt

4 ounces grated white Cheddar (aged)

4 ounces crumbled goat's cheese (soft)

2 boxes (16 ounce) dried elbow macaroni (gluten free)

1 large lacinato kale bunch, (stems removed and leaves cut into ribbons)

Directions

Set a large pot with salted water over high heat and bring to boil. Add in the macaroni and stir for about a minute to ensure the pieces won't stick together. Cook for 8 minutes and remove from heat. Put the Cheddar, kale and goat's cheese in the bottom of a large bowl. Remove the macaroni from heat using a slotted spoon after the 8 minutes while still soft but has a bite, and place it on top of the goat cheese and kale mixture then pour in about 1/3 cup of the water used to cook macaroni. Let everything sit for around five minutes then mix thoroughly and serve.

17. Rice & Lentil Salad

Rice & Lentil Salad

Servings: 4

Ingredients

2 cups of cooked brown rice

1 tablespoon Dijon mustard

2 tablespoons extra virgin olive oil

1 tablespoon shallot, finely chopped

¼ teaspoon salt

¼ teaspoon freshly ground pepper

½ teaspoon paprika (smoked is preferred)

2 tablespoons red-wine or sherry vinegar

2 tablespoons freshly chopped parsley

1 diced carrot

1 (15 ounce) can of lentils, rinsed or 1 1/3 cups of cooked lentils

Directions

Combine shallot, paprika, vinegar, olive oil, salt, mustard and pepper in a large bowl. Add in cooked rice, carrot, lentils and parsley and stir to combine. Serve while warm.

18. Butternut Squash Salad

Butternut Squash Salad

Servings: 4

Ingredients

50g of Puy lentils

50g wild brown rice

50g of dried cranberry

25g of pumpkin seeds

Lemon juice (freshly squeezed from 1 lemon)

1 teaspoon virgin olive oil

1 butternut squash (deseeded, diced and peeled)

1 head of broccoli cut in florets

Directions

Preheat the oven to 200 degrees C then spread the squash on a wide baking sheet, drizzle oil over and bake for about 30 minutes or until it softens. Put the lentils and rice in boiling salted water and cook for 20 minutes adding the broccoli towards the final minutes of cooking. Drain, stir in pumpkin seeds and cranberries with some seasoning. Add in the squash then pour over the lemon juice and serve warm.

Gluten Free Dinner Recipes

19. Chickpea Bajane

Chickpea Bajane

Servings: 4

Ingredients

4 chopped, garlic cloves

4 teaspoons of extra virgin olive oil (divided)

1 cup of water

2 cups of thinly sliced leek

1 cup raw quinoa

5 ½ teaspoons fresh thyme (divided)

1 teaspoon of salt (divided)

2 cups of organic vegetable broth (divided)

1 minced garlic clove

½ teaspoon of fennel seeds

1 tablespoon lemon juice, fresh

¼ teaspoon freshly grounded pepper

1 (6 oz) bunch fresh baby spinach

½ cup of white wine

1 ¾ cups slices of carrot (¼ inch thick)

2 ½ cups fennel bulb, sliced

1 (15 oz) can chickpeas (no salt added, rinsed and drained)

Directions

Heat 2 teaspoons extra virgin olive oil in a large saucepan over medium-high heat. A add in 1 minced garlic clove to the pan and sauté for a minute. In equal proportions of 1 cup each, add broth, water and quinoa then thyme and salt. Reduce the heat, cover and boil for 15 minutes or until the quinoa is tender and liquid is absorbed. Remove from the heat and fluff with a fork. Over medium heat, place 1 teaspoon of olive oil in a Dutch oven, add 4 chopped garlic cloves to the pan and leek and sauté for 5 minutes or until tender. Add carrot, fennel bulb, the remainder 1 teaspoon of virgin olive oil and fennel seeds and sauté them for 10 minutes or until the vegetables turn golden. Add some wine and cook for about 3 minutes before stirring in 2 teaspoons thyme, broth and chickpeas then cook for another minute or until its thoroughly heated. Remove from heat, stir in some pepper, salt, lemon juice and spinach. To serve, place 2/3 cup-size quinoa into 4 bowls and top each with 1 ½ cups chickpea mix then sprinkle with some thyme each.

20. Pork Chops with Peach Barbecue Sauce

Pork Chops with Peach Barbecue Sauce

Servings: 4

Ingredients

4 center-cut, bone-in pork chops (trimmed, ½ -3/4 inch thick)

2 tablespoons of cider vinegar

2 tablespoons fresh ginger, finely chopped

¼ teaspoon freshly ground pepper + more to taste

2 tablespoons honey

1 medium size tomato (quartered and seeded)

2 ripe peaches (pitted and quartered)

¼ cup of brown sugar (firmly packed)

2 cups of boiling water

¼ cup plus ½ teaspoons kosher salt (divided)

3 cups of ice cubes

1 tablespoon of canola oil

½ cup of Vidalia chopped onion

Directions

Put brown sugar and ¼ cup of salt in a medium heat-proof bowl then add in boiling water while stirring to ensure that the sugar and salt are completely dissolved. Add in ice cubes and then stir for cooling then put in pork chops, then cover with a lid and then refrigerate for 30minutes – 4 hours. Blend tomato, peaches and vinegar in a food processor until smooth. Pre-heat oil in a medium size saucepan over medium-high heat,

30 minutes before getting ready to cook pork chops. Add in onion stirring sparingly to cook until browned. Add in ginger as you stir until fragrant. Now add in the remaining ½ teaspoon salt, honey, peach blend and pepper, boil then lower the heat to a simmer. Cook until it reduces by half, around 20-25 minutes. Reserve ¼ cup of the sauce for basting the pork chops and keep the remaining sauce in the saucepan to retain warmth until ready to serve.

Preheat the grill to medium. Remove the pork chops from the brine, rinse well and dry completely with paper towels. Use ¼ teaspoon of the pepper to season the pork chops and brush both sides with the reserved sauce. Grill pork-chops turning them a little until a thermometer stuck at the center registers 145 degrees F, estimated 2-4 minutes each side. Remove from grill and onto a plate, cover with foil and allow to stand for 5 minutes. Serve with the warm peach barbeque sauce if desired.

21. Indian-Spiced Salmon

Indian-Spiced Salmon

Servings: 4

Ingredients

½ teaspoon ground ginger

¼ teaspoon ground turmeric

½ teaspoon ground coriander

½ teaspoon garam masala

4 (6 oz) skinless salmon fillets

Dash of Kosher salt

Cooking spray

Dash of Red pepper

Directions

Preheat the broiler and combine ginger, turmeric, garam masala, coriander, salt and pepper. Rub this mixture over fillets evenly then place the fillets on a baking sheet or broiler pan coated with cooking spray. Cover this with foil and then broil for 7 minutes. Remove foil and broil for another 4 minutes or until the desired degree of doneness is achieved.

22. Herbes de Provence-Crusted Lamb Chops

Herbes de Provence-Crusted Lamb Chops

Servings: 4

Ingredients

2 tablespoons Dijon mustard

1 tablespoon dried herbs (herbes de provence)

½ teaspoon kosher salt

1 minced, garlic clove

¼ teaspoon black pepper (freshly ground)

8 oz chops of trimmed lamb loin

Cooking spray

Directions

Preheat the grill to medium-high heat then combine Dijon mustard, black pepper, garlic olive, salt and herbs rubbing evenly over both sides of the lamb. Coat the grill rack with cooking spray and place the lamb on top. Grill for about 4 minutes on each side until it is done.

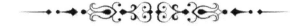

23. Chicken Tacos with Mango-Avocado Salsa

Chicken Tacos with Mango-Avocado Salsa

Servings: 4

Ingredients

¼ teaspoon red pepper (ground)

1 teaspoon of garlic powder

1 teaspoon paprika

1 teaspoon onion powder

4 (6 ounce) boneless, skinless chicken breasts (halves)

1 ½ teaspoons olive oil

¾ teaspoon salt, divided

½ cup peeled avocado (diced)

½ cup of peeled mango (diced)

1/3 cup of onion (chopped)

2 tablespoons fresh cilantro (chopped)

2 tablespoons lime juice (fresh)

1 tablespoon of minced jalapeno pepper

½ cup of chopped tomato

4 (8 inch) brown rice tortillas

Directions

Preheat a non-stick skillet over medium-high heat. Combine paprika, onion powder, garlic and red pepper then stir in ½ teaspoon of salt and rub over chicken. Add oil to the pan, swirl to coat then add the chicken and cook for 4 minutes on each side or until done.

Meanwhile combine mango, avocado, tomato, onion, oil, cilantro and lime juice then stir in the remaining ¼ teaspoon of salt. After the chicken has cooked for 4 minutes, transfer from the pan and allow it to stand for 5 minutes. Slice into ¼-inch thick pieces. Serve with gluten free tortillas and salsa.

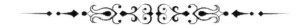

24. Gluten-Free Glazed Meat Loaf

Gluten-Free Glazed Meat Loaf

Servings: 4

Ingredients

Meat loaf:

½ cup size gluten free crackers, crushed

1 ½ lean beef

2 tablespoons milk

2 tablespoons ketchup (gluten free)

½ teaspoon salt

1 tablespoon Dijon Mustard (gluten free)

1 teaspoon sage leaves (dried)

¼ teaspoon pepper

1 small onion finely chopped (¼ cup)

1 egg

Glaze:

1 tablespoon brown sugar (packed)

1 teaspoon gluten free Dijon mustard

½ cup gluten free ketchup

Directions

Preheat the oven to 350 degrees F and combine all the meat loaf ingredients in a large bowl. Spread this mixture in 8 x 4 inch ungreased loaf pan. Combine all the glaze ingredients in a smaller bowl, mix evenly and spread on the meat loaf. Bake the meat loaf uncovered for 60-75 minutes or until a thermometer put in the center of the loaf indicates 160 degrees F. Remove from oven and allow for 5 minutes cooling before slicing. Serve as desired.

25. Gluten-Free Skillet Chicken Divan

Gluten-Free Skillet Chicken Divan

Servings: 4

Ingredients

4 skinless, boneless chicken breasts

1 tablespoon margarine or butter

2 tablespoons of Dijon mustard

¼ teaspoon salt

1/8 teaspoon pepper

1 cup uncooked brown rice (gluten free)

3 cups frozen broccoli florets (thawed)

½ cup (2 ounce) American cheese or Cheddar (shredded)

Water

Directions

Melt the butter in a 10-inch skillet (non-stick) over medium-high heat then add chicken. Cook for about 1-2 minutes on each side or until golden. Remove chicken from the skillet and add salt, pepper, mustard and water to the skillet stirring with a wire whisk until thoroughly blended. Bring to a boil and stir in the brown rice. Bring to a boil then place broccoli and the chicken pieces over the rice. Reduce heat to low, cover and simmer for about 10 more minutes. Sprinkle with some cheese, cover and let it cool for 5 minutes.

26. Italian Hamburger Deep Dish

Italian Hamburger Deep Dish

Servings: 8

Ingredients

1 lb lean ground beef (at least 80%)

1/8 teaspoon pepper

1 teaspoon salt

1 finely chopped clove garlic

2 2/3 cups of water

¼ cup margarine or butter (low fat)

1 teaspoon salt (optional)

2/3 cups milk

2 tablespoons minced onion

1 teaspoon oregano leaves (dried)

2 cups mashed potatoes

3-4 medium sliced tomatoes

4 ounces shredded and sliced mozzarella cheese

Directions

Preheat oven to 350 degrees F, then butter 11 x 7 inch glass baking dish. In a 10-inch skillet, add the beef, pepper and 1 tablespoon of garlic over medium heat stirring sparingly until the beef is browned. Drain and leave alone.

In a 3-quart saucepan, bring water, 1 teaspoon salt, butter, oregano and onion to a boil. Remove from heat then add in dry potatoes and milk until moistened. Let it stand for 30 seconds or until the liquid dissolves then whip with a fork until fluffy. Layer half of the potato mix on a baking dish, then add a layer of half of the tomatoes and beef then top with remaining potato mix and tomatoes and then sprinkle some cheese. Bake in the oven without cover for about 30 minutes or until bubbly.

27. Prosciutto-Wrapped Basil Shrimp

Prosciutto-Wrapped Basil Shrimp

Servings: 2

Ingredients

20 large deveined shrimp (peeled, frozen, thawed)

¼ teaspoon red pepper flakes

1/8 teaspoon freshly ground pepper (black)

1 teaspoon extra virgin olive oil

1 tablespoon fresh basil (chopped)

½ teaspoon kosher salt

½ teaspoon lemon zest

8 lemon wedges (to serve)

10 (4 ounce) thinly sliced prosciutto

Cooking spray

Directions

Preheat broiler and combine basil, shrimp, olive oil, salt, red pepper flakes, black pepper and zest. Mix thoroughly and set aside. Spread the prosciutto slices on a flexible workspace and cut them halfway to have 20 slices. Wrap the prosciuttos round each shrimp with the tail hanging out then put the shrimp on an 8-inch skewer. Do the same with the rest of the shrimp to have 4 skewers with 5 shrimp each. Lightly coat a broiling pan with cooking spray and place the skewers on top then broil the shrimp on each side for about 2 minutes. Remove from broiler and serve hot with lemon wedges if desired.

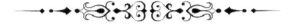

28. Nam Sod

Nam Sod

Servings: 4

Ingredients

1/3 cup green onions, finely chopped

½ cup red onion, cut in thin vertical slices

3 tablespoons fresh limejuice

Cooking spray

1 pound of ground turkey breast

1 ½ tablespoons fish sauce

1 tablespoon fresh ginger (minced, peeled)

1 teaspoon chili paste with garlic

2 tablespoons dry, roasted peanuts

½ small size green cabbage, separated into leaves

Directions

Heat a large non-stick skillet over medium heat then coat it with cooking spray and place the turkey on the pan. Cook for about 4 minutes or until it's done. Transfer turkey from the frying pan to a platter and allow it to cool. Mix the onions with limejuice, ginger, fish sauce, chili paste and roasted peanuts in a medium size bowl and allow it to stand for 10 minutes. Place turkey in the mixture and sprinkle with some peanuts. Serve with cabbage leaves.

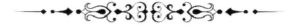

Gluten Free Salads

29. Mexican Spinach Salad

Mexican Spinach Salad

Servings: 2

Ingredients

¼ cup of olive oil

1 tablespoon lime zest

1 teaspoon salt

1 tablespoon agave or honey

4 cups baby spinach (fresh)

1 cup canned or fresh corn

1 cup grape tomatoes (halved)

1 cup canned or fresh corn

1 cup diced avocado

1 cup of canned, drained and rinsed black beans

1/3 cup chopped cilantro

Fresh black pepper

Directions

To make the dressing: In a lidded jar, add olive oil, lime zest, lime juice, honey, salt and vinegar then seal and shake thoroughly. Freeze in the refrigerator for about 2 hours or until it's ready for serving.

In a wide mixing bowl, add spinach, drizzle some of the dressing and then toss in the tomatoes, corn, black beans, cilantro and avocado. Add some more or less of the dressing and toss. Season with salt and pepper then serve with tortilla chips if desired.

30. Gluten Free Strawberry Spinach Salad with Strawberry Vinaigrette Dressing

Gluten Free Strawberry Spinach Salad with Strawberry Vinaigrette Dressing

Servings: 4

Ingredients

Salad:

1 bag (8-ounces) baby spinach

8 thinly sliced scallions (greens and whites)

1 ½ cups fresh strawberries, stemmed and sliced in halves

A handful of Caramelized (optional) walnuts or pecans

1 cup Blue cheese, goat cheese or feta cheese

For dressing:

8 large, sliced strawberries

2 teaspoons agave nectar or honey

6 tablespoons extra virgin oil

5 tablespoons balsamic vinegar

6 tablespoons virgin olive oil (extra)

Directions

Add all the main (salad) ingredients above in a wide bowl and add some of the dressing that follows to taste then toss.

To make the Dressing: Whisk all the ingredients for the dressing together until thoroughly mixed. Use a food processor if desired as this will result in a much creamier dressing.

31. Cucumber Salad

Cucumber Salad

Servings: 2

Ingredients

½ teaspoon Celtic sea salt

2 peeled cucumbers

½ cup apple cider vinegar

Directions

Cut the cucumber into ¼ inch cucumber slices and place in a mediumsize bowl. Dress with vinegar and sprinkle with the Celtic sea salt. Serve for two.

32. Vegan Gluten-Free Skordalia Dip

Vegan Gluten-Free Skordalia Dip

Servings: 1

Ingredients

6-12 cloves of garlic finely chopped

4 medium size organic potatoes (washed, scrubbed and not peeled)

2 tablespoons white vinegar

5 tablespoons lemon juice or as desired much

1 cup slivered or blanched almonds

Freshly ground pepper

½ cup of extra virgin oil (cold pressed)

1 bunch of finely chopped coriander

Celtic sea salt (to taste)

Directions

Wash and scrub the medium size potatoes then cover with cold water in a large bowl with a generous dash of Celtic sea salt. Bring to a boil and simmer for 30 minutes until cooked. Mince the garlic and then puree in a food processor together with almonds and olive oil to have a garlic paste. Drain the potatoes, gently remove the skin and mash gently. Fold through about half of the garlic paste gently then sparingly add the lemon juice, salt, vinegar and pepper to taste. Finally stir in a little of the freshly chopped cilantro, chives or parsley. Serve immediately.

33. Summer Kidney Bean and Corn Salad

Summer Kidney Bean and Corn Salad

Servings: 6

Ingredients

155g of fresh or frozen sweet corn kernels

1 small size onion

1 halved punnet cherry tomato

400 grams red kidney beans (canned, drained and rinsed)

2 tablespoons lime juice

1 teaspoon lemon zest

1 tablespoon olive oil (more or less)

Freshly ground black pepper and salt to taste

A large bunch of fresh, finely chopped basil

Directions

In a large bowl, toss the red kidney beans, sweet corns, tomatoes, lime juice, onion and lemon zest. Drizzle with some olive oil then season with pepper and salt. Add in basil just before you serve.

34. Spinach Salad with Home-made Salad Dressing

Spinach Salad with Home-made Salad Dressing

Servings: 4-6

Ingredients

1 medium bunch of fresh spinach, washed and dried

1 cup red onions, thinly sliced

4 slices of cooked, chopped bacon (gluten free)

1 cup of mushrooms, thinly sliced

¼ teaspoon smoked paprika (if desired)

3 finely chopped hard-boiled eggs

Dressing:

1 cup extra virgin oil

1/3 cup ketchup (gluten free)

¼ cup apple cider vinegar

½ or ¾ cup sugar or less

1 teaspoon Worcestershire sauce

Directions

Dressing: Put the dressing ingredients in a medium size bowl and whisk until the sugar dissolves and the dressing is glossy and smooth. Store in a lidded container and refrigerate.

Salad: Cut the spinach leaves into bite size pieces. Toss together with sliced onions, chopped gluten-free bacon and mushrooms. Add chopped eggs as topping and dust with some smoked paprika if desired. Pour the refrigerated dressing and serve.

35. Sweet and Creamy Broccoli Salad

Sweet and Creamy Broccoli Salad

Servings: 6

Ingredients

Salad:

¼ cup chopped red onion

¼ cup sunflower seeds

½ cup thinly sliced, sun-dried tomatoes

7 strips uncured beef bacon, cooked and chopped

¼ cup dried currants

6 cups fresh broccoli florets, steamed for about 3 minutes

Dressing:

½ cup of canola, egg free-mayonnaise or olive oil

2 tablespoons raw apple cider vinegar

1 tablespoon mustard (gluten-free)

1 tablespoon honey, unpasteurized

Handful of fresh parsley

Directions

Fry bacon as instructed on the package and be sure to cook until it is crisp. Beef bacon is often preferred as it's much higher in protein, has less fat and is easy to digest. Once it is cooked, place on a plate lined with paper towels. Pat it dry and break into small pieces. Now add the bacon, red onions, currants, sun dried tomatoes and sunflower seeds to the broccoli bowl and in a separate smaller bowl, mix the dressing ingredients and stir until thoroughly incorporated. Pour the dressing over the broccoli mixture and stir to evenly coat. Sprinkle fresh parsley to taste then serve.

36. Apple, Quinoa & lentil Salad with Maple Pork

Apple, Quinoa & lentil Salad with Maple Pork

Servings: 4

Ingredients

2 tablespoons lemon juice

2 teaspoons extra virgin oil

1 tablespoon maple syrup

¼ teaspoon dried chili flakes

2 small red apples cut into wedges

1 large red onion, cut into thin wedges

½ cup size coarsely chopped fresh mint leaves

½ cup coarsely chopped continental parsley leaves

450g pork fillet

¾ cup of water plus 1 tablespoon of water

½ cup rinsed quinoa

400g can of brown lentils (drained and rinsed)

2 celery sticks, cut thinly

Lemon wedges (to serve)

Baby herbs (to serve)

Directions

Heat oven up to 160-180 degrees C, then line a baking tray with some baking powder. Place the apple and onions on the tray and drizzle with olive oil. Toss to mix and roast for about 20 minutes or until golden and tender. In the meantime, mix syrup, half of the lemon juice, a tablespoon of water and chili in a bowl. Heat a non-stick oven proof frying pan over medium heat. Sparingly spray pork with olive oil, season with salt and pepper and cook while tossing for 5 minutes until brown. Remove from heat, pour the lemon juice mixture and roast for 10-12 minutes or until thoroughly cooked. Remove it from the pan and place on a plate for cooking for about 5 minutes. Slice the pork and allow pan juices to stand for 5 minutes to allow thickening.

Place ¾ cup water and quinoa in a small size saucepan over medium heat then bring to boil. Reduce heat to low, simmer while stirring occasionally for about 8-10 minutes or until the quinoa is tender and water is absorbed. Combine the quinoa, lentils, apple mixture, mint, celery and the remaining lemon juice in a bowl and season. Share among 4-5 plates; top each with pork and pan juices then sprinkle with herbs. Serve the salad with lemon wedges.

Gluten Free Desserts

37. Chewy Caramel Apple Cookies

Chewy Caramel Apple Cookies

Servings: 36

Ingredients

½ cup plus 2 tablespoons softened unsalted butter

6.75 oz gluten free flour like almond flour, rice flour or coconut flour

2 tablespoons milk

¾ teaspoon baking soda

¼ teaspoon salt

2 tablespoons milk

2 tablespoons water

1 ½ cup old-fashioned rolled oats (gluten-free)

1 large egg

¾ teaspoon vanilla extract

20 caramel candies

½ cup plus 2 tablespoons brown sugar (packed)

Directions

Preheat the oven to 325 degrees F then beat brown sugar and butter with a mixer until creamy. Add in milk, egg and vanilla and beat for 2 more minutes until it's light and fluffy. Combine flour, salt and baking soda in a medium bowl and stir with a whisk. Pour in oats and add this mixture to the butter mixture while beating at low speed until well blended. Add the apples and stir.

Place 1 ½ tablespoons of dough about 2 inches apart on baking sheet lined with parchment paper. Bake at 325 degrees F for 14 minutes or until golden then transfer the cookies to wire racks to cool completely. Place water and caramel candies in a small size saucepan and cook over low heat while stirring to smoothen for 7 minutes. Remove from heat and sparingly drizzle warm glaze over the cookies. Allow caramel to set completely, i.e. about 15 minutes then transfer to an airtight container and store for up to 5 days.

38. Hazelnut-Brown-Butter Brownies

Hazelnut-Brown-Butter Brownies

Servings: 20

Ingredients

1 cup plus 2 tablespoons unsweetened cocoa powder

7 ounces hazelnuts

12 ounces bittersweet chocolate

1 teaspoon salt

3 cups of sugar

1 tablespoon of instant coffee (dissolved in 1 tablespoon hot water)

6 large eggs

4 sticks (1 pound) unsalted butter

Directions

Preheat oven to 325 degrees F and line a baking pan with foil. Spread the hazelnuts on a pie plate then toast until the skins blister and are fragrant then transfer to a kitchen towel. Rub off the skins and allow to cool completely before transferring to a food processor. Add the salt, cocoa and ½ cup of the sugar and then pulse until it is finely ground. Cook the butter in a saucepan over moderate heat while shaking the pan occasionally until golden and nutty smelling. Remove from heat, add chocolate while stirring until smooth then allow it to cool.

Using an electric mixer, beat the eggs, coffee and the remaining 2 ½ cups of sugar in a large bowl for about 5 minutes. Add in the chocolate-butter mix, the cocoa-hazelnut mix and beat to mix. Scrape the butter in the pan and bake for up to 50 minutes until the top is glossy. Allow the brownie to cool on a rack then refrigerate until it is chilled. Lift the brownie out of the baking pan and peel off the foil then cut into 20 pieces. Serve with ice cream if desired.

39. Flourless Peanut Butter Cookies

Flourless Peanut Butter Cookies

Servings: 1

Ingredients

1 egg

1 cup of white sugar

1 cup of peanut butter

Directions

Preheat the oven to 180 degrees F. Mix the ingredients above and place teaspoonfuls of the mix on a cookie sheet. Bake for 8 minutes, remove from oven and allow to cool. Serve with milk.

40. Chantal's New York Cheesecake

Chantal's New York Cheesecake

Servings: 8

Ingredients

1 tablespoon vanilla extract

2 tablespoons butter, melted

¾ cup of milk

¼ cup coconut flour

1 cup of sour cream

1 ½ cups of white sugar

15 crushed gluten free graham cracker crumbs

4 (8ounce) packages cream cheese

8 eggs

Directions

Preheat the oven to 350 degrees F and grease a 9 inch spring form pan. Mix graham crackers in a medium size bowl with melted butter. Press this onto the button of spring-form pan. Mix cream cheese with sugar until smooth in a large bowl, blend in milk and then beat in the eggs one at a time stirring sparingly to incorporate. Pour in the sour cream, flour, and vanilla and then stir until smooth. Pour filling into the prepared crust. Bake this in your preheated oven for 1 hour, turn the oven off and allow the cake to cool while in the oven for about 5-6 hours with the door tightly closed to prevent cracking. Once cooled, you can chill until ready to serve.

41. Piña Colada Cheesecake Bars

Piña Colada Cheesecake Bars

Servings: 16

Ingredients

1 cup gluten-free graham crackers, crushed

2 tablespoons melted butter

1 tablespoon water

1 tablespoons canola oil

2 tablespoons turbinado sugar

2 tablespoons coconut flour

½ teaspoon ground ginger

½ cup sugar

1 cup 2% low-fat cottage cheese

1 ½ tablespoons grated lemon rind

¼ cup (2 ounces) fat free, softened cream cheese (block-style)

1 tablespoon pineapple juice

1 cup of chopped pineapple (fresh)

¼ cup unsweetened coconut (toasted, shredded)

½ teaspoon vanilla extract

¾ cup egg substitute

Cooking spray

Dash of Salt

Directions

Preheat the oven to 175 degrees C. Combine the graham crackers, coconut flour, turbinado sugar and ground ginger in a bowl. Add butter, 1 tablespoon water and oil then toss to mix. Transfer the mix into the bottom of an 8" metal baking pan coated with cooking spray and square in shape. Bake for 10 minutes at 175 degrees C then cool thoroughly on a wire rack. Put cottage cheese, sugar, grated lemon rind, pineapple juice, vanilla extract, lemon juice and cream cheese in a food processor and blend until smooth. Add the egg substitute and continue blending to smoothen. Spread the cheese mix over the cooled crust and bake for 35 minutes at 170 degrees C until set. Transfer to a wire rack for ten minutes and allow to cool. Refrigerate for about 2 hours or until completely chilled. Top with coconut and pineapple then cut into 16 bars.

42. Flourless Chocolate Cake

Flourless Chocolate Cake

Servings: 10

Ingredients

1 cup sugar

1 ½ cups of heavy cream

½ cup of sour cream

¼ cup of confectioner's sugar

1 cup unsalted butter plus 2 tablespoons cut into pieces

¼ cup plus 2 tablespoons unsweetened cocoa powder

8 ounces bitter-sweet chopped chocolate

5 large eggs

Directions

Heat the oven up to 175 degrees C then grease a 9-inch pan and dust with cocoa powder. Heat the butter in a medium-size saucepan with ¼ cup heavy cream in medium-low heat until the butter melts. Add in the chocolate while stirring until it is melted and smooth. Remove from heat and set aside.

In a medium-size bowl, beat in the eggs, add cocoa powder and granulated sugar then whisk before pouring into the chocolate mixture. Transfer the mix into the prepared pan and then bake until set and puffed, about 35-40 minutes. Allow the cake to cool while still in the pan for about an hour then run a knife carefully around the edges of the cake just before unmolding.

Beat the remaining heavy cream (1 cup) with the sour cream and confectioners' sugar using an electric mixer until it forms soft peaks. Use the confectioners' sugar to dust the cake, cut and serve it with the whipped cream.

43. Pumpkin Brulee

Pumpkin Brulee

Servings: 12

Ingredients

4 cups of heavy cream

¼ teaspoon salt

¼ teaspoon ground ginger

1/8 teaspoon ground cloves

1 teaspoon ground cinnamon

2 teaspoons vanilla extract

¼ cup brown sugar

¾ cup plus ¼ cup white sugar

1 cup canned pumpkin puree

16 medium eggs yolks

Directions

Preheat the oven to 165 degrees C. Using a large heavy saucepan, heat the cream and vanilla and bring to a boil. Beat the egg yolks in a bowl and mix with white sugar, brown sugar, cinnamon, ginger, salt, pumpkin and cloves. Pour 1 cup of the mixed cream into the egg mixture while stirring in continuous motion. Pour the resultant mixture into the saucepan and whisk continuously for a minute. Pour the mix into ramekins and arrange them on a baking sheet. Bake in the preheated oven for about 15 minutes until set then refrigerate for about 4-6 hours. Sprinkle 1 teaspoon sugar on top of each crème brulee. Using your oven's broiler, caramelize the sugar; this might take around 2-3 minutes. Serve as soon as it is ready.

Gluten Free Smoothies

44. Cranberry and Raspberry Smoothie

Cranberry and Raspberry Smoothie

Servings: 5

Ingredients

200ml cranberry juice

100ml milk

175 gram frozen raspberries (defrosted)

200ml natural yogurt

1 tablespoon caster sugar

Mint sprigs to serve

Directions

Pour all the ingredients into a blender and blend until smooth.

Pour into 5 glasses and garnish with fresh mint

45. Raspberry-Avocado Smoothie

Raspberry-Avocado Smoothie

Servings: 2

Ingredients

½ cup of frozen raspberries (not thawed)

¾ cup of raspberry juice

¾ cup orange juice

1 avocado peeled and pitted

Directions

Mix raspberries, avocado, raspberry juice and orange juice in a blender or food processor and mix until soft. Pour into two glasses and serve immediately.

46. Berry- Coconut Smoothie

Berry- Coconut Smoothie

Servings: 1

Ingredients

½ cup of low-fat plain yogurt

½ cup of raspberries, blueberries, strawberries or black berries (or any other berries)

½ cup of coconut milk

½ cup vanilla or unflavored whey protein powder

½ teaspoon coconut extract

1 tablespoon ground flax seeds

4 ice-cubes

Directions

Place all the ingredients above in a blender or food processor. Blend until it is smooth and serve immediately.

47. Açaí Smoothie

Açaí Smoothie

Servings: 2

Ingredients

1 medium banana

100g raw, unsweetened açaí pulp

50g frozen pineapple

100g of strawberries

250ml orange or mango juice

1 tablespoon agave honey or nectar

Directions

Place the ingredients in a blender and blend until you obtain a smooth consistency. If it is too thick, add more orange or mango juice and serve in two large glasses.

48. Banana Smoothie

Banana Smoothie

Servings: 2

Ingredients

½ cup 1% low-fat milk

1 tablespoon of honey

1/8 tablespoon of ground nutmeg

1 cup 2% low fat plain Greek yoghurt

1 large ripe banana (frozen)

½ cup of ice (crushed)

Directions

Add milk, honey, ground nutmeg and crushed ice in a blender and process for about two minutes. Add the Greek yoghurt and blend until smooth. Pour into two tall glasses and serve immediately.

49. Tropical Tea Smoothies

Tropical Tea Smoothies

Servings: 4

Ingredients

1 cup of boiling water

2 cups of decaffeinated tea bags

1 tablespoon honey

1 small banana

1 cup of ice cubes

1 can (8 ounces) crushed pineapple juice (natural, un-drained)

Directions

Pour boiled water straight from the boiling kettle over Lipton cup-size tea bags in a teapot and cover for 5 minutes to brew then chill. Process tea, banana, pineapple and ice cubes in a blender until smoothened. Serve in four tall glasses and garnish with fresh pineapple wedges if desired.

50. Spiced Apple Pie Smoothie

Spiced Apple Pie Smoothie

Servings: 2

Ingredients

1 cup yoghurt (vanilla or plain)

1 teaspoon cinnamon

1 banana, medium size (previously frozen if possible)

1 ½ cups apple juice

¼ cup milk (optional, omit to retain a thicker smoothie)

½ teaspoon vanilla extract

2 cups ice (optional or if necessary)

Pinch of nutmeg and cardamom

Sugar or sweetener to taste (optional or if necessary)

Directions

Mix all ingredients but ice in a Vita-mix or wide blender and blend until smooth and creamy making sure any incorporated sweetener has dissolved. Pour ice into the smoothie if desired bearing in mind it will reduce thickness a bit. Freeze or refrigerate for a while or if time permits for best results. Serve

51. Spinach Smoothie

Spinach Smoothie

Servings: 1

Ingredients

1 tablespoon honey

1 cup almond milk

1 ripe banana

1 cup spinach leaves, loosely packed

Directions

Put all ingredients in a blender and blend until smooth.

Gluten Free Drinks and Cocktails

52. No Sugar Iced Coffee

No Sugar Iced Coffee

Servings: 2

Ingredients

½ cup low fat milk

½ cup sweetened condensed milk

Whipped cream (optional)

2 cups strong coffee

4 cups of ice cubes

Directions

Mix all the above ingredients in a blender or food processor and blend until it's finally smooth. Add whipped cream topping if you like.

53. Mocha Cocktail

Mocha Cocktail

Servings: 1

Ingredients

Cold brewed, un-flavored coffee

2-3 ounces heavy whipping cream

½ cup of ice

½ ounce Fernet Liqueur

Sugar to taste

½ oz. Homemade

Unsweetened cocoa powder (gluten free)

Hot fudge sauce (gluten free)

A scoop of chocolate or coffee ice cream (gluten free; optional)

Whipped cream (gluten free; optional)

Directions

Make instant or brewed coffee and add sugar like you would while drinking, then refrigerate for cooling. In a Martini shaker, add ice, Fernet, chocolate liqueur, cream and shake it until well blended. Immerse the frame of a glass into water and then into a bowl of cocoa powder. Add some hot fudge sauce on the base of a glass in stripes or decorative design then pour the cocktail into the same glass leaving room for the sweetened coffee and ice cream. If desired add the sweetened coffee or ice cream or both to taste.

54. Cosmopolitan Recipe with a Twist

Cosmopolitan Recipe with a Twist

Servings: 3

Ingredients

1/3 cup or 2 shots homemade orange liqueur

1 cup of vodka

½ cup pomegranate juice

¼ cup of fresh lime juice

½ cup of cranberry juice

4 (2-inch) orange peels or lemon (curled)

Directions

Mix all the ingredients and chill in the fridge.

Prior to serving, halfway fill a martini shaker with ice and some Cosmo mix. Shake and pour into martini glasses. Garnish using a curled citrus peel and serve.

55. Cidertini

Cidertini

Servings: 1

Ingredients

¼ cup gluten free vodka

1 teaspoon Sugar

Cinnamon (to taste)

¼ cup apple cider vinegar

Splash of GF vanilla

Butterscotch swirl

Directions

Mix all the items and shake with ice. Pour into a glass layered with crushed ginger snaps and sugar or cinnamon

56. Champagne Punch

Champagne Punch

Servings: 20

Ingredients

1 (12 ounce) can of frozen orange juice concentrate, thawed

1 (2 liter) bottle of chilled champagne

1 (2 liter) bottle of chilled ginger ale

1 (12 ounce) can of frozen limeade concentrate, thawed

1 (12 ounce) can of frozen lemonade concentrate, thawed

Directions

Mix the concentrates in a punch bowl without adding any water. Add in the Gingerale and stir followed by Champagne after which do not stir. Serve

57. Savannah Cocktail Recipe With Absinthe

Savannah Cocktail Recipe With Absinthe

Servings: 1

Ingredients

1 ounce of water

1 ounce fresh lemon juice

1 ounce Pernod Absinthe (Darjeeling infused)

1 ounce peach syrup

Directions

Mix the ingredients then shake well for about 10 seconds and drain into a chilled glass. Garnish with lemon wheel and straw. Add the Darjeeling tea to Pernod and allow cooling for 30-60 minutes depending on desired concentrate. Serve into cocktail glasses.

58. Escape from Alcatraz Cocktail

Escape from Alcatraz Cocktail

Servings: 2

Ingredients

1 teaspoon fresh ginger, grated

1 tablespoon lemon juice (freshly squeezed)

2 ounces rye whiskey

Ice cubes

3 orange slices

1 ounce Cointreau

Directions

Muddle the orange and ginger slices in a cocktail shaker and add lemon juice. Add the Cointreau and Whiskey shaking well with ice. Strain into an ice-filled glass and garnish with a slice of orange.

59. Gluten Free Virgin Watermelon Cocktail

Gluten Free Virgin Watermelon Cocktail

Servings: 1

Ingredients

½ (large, 3lbs), seedless watermelon cubed and rind removed.

2 thinly sliced lemons

Directions

Squash watermelon cubes in a blender or food processor and strain through a fine mesh strainer if need be. Squeeze in lemon juice and then garnish with a lemon slice. Serve over ice or chilled.

60. Gluten Free Hawaiian Cocktail

Gluten Free Hawaiian Cocktail

Servings: 2

Ingredients

2 pineapple wedges to garnish

2 maraschino cherries for garnishing

6 ounces fresh pineapple juice

1 ½ ounces rum

2 ounces gluten-free sweet and sour mix

1 ½ ounces orange liquor

Directions

Add all the ingredients into a blender with some ice and blend until the ice is crushed then pour into a glass and garnish with a cherry and pineapple wedge.

Conclusion

Embracing a gluten-free diet is not easy. However, once you get the hang of it, it even becomes easier. The good thing is that you also get to enjoy your favorite meals like cookies and cakes with the difference being the use of substitutes hence, no need to feel deprived.

Thank you again for purchasing this book!

I hope this book was able to help you to learn about some recipes to try out.

Finally, if you enjoyed this book, would you be kind enough to leave a review for this book on Amazon? It'd be greatly appreciated!

Thank you and good luck!

Katharine Jackson